SUS

Wit & Humour

CHELSEA LAVANT

BRADWELL
BOOKS

Published by Bradwell Books

9 Orgreave Close Sheffield S13 9NP

Email: books@bradwellbooks.co.uk

Compiled by Chelsea Lavant

British Library Cataloguing in Publication Data: a catalogue record for this book is available from the British Library.

1st Edition

ISBN: 9781909914131

Print: Gomer Press, Llandysul, Ceredigion SA44 4JL

Design by: jenksdesign@yahoo.co.uk

Illustrations: ©Tim O'Brien 2013

"My wife and I went on a sail making holiday in Sussex last summer."

"Firle?"

"At the end of the process, yes, but mainly sewing."

"I got a wine gum stuck to my shoe when I was rambling through a lovely village in East Sussex."

"Maynards Green?"

"Couldn't tell—it was squashed and covered in mud."

The leader of a vegetarian society just couldn't control himself any more. He simply needed to try some pork, just to see what it tasted like. So one day he told his members he was going away for a break. He left town and headed to the nearest restaurant. After sitting down, he ordered a roasted pig, and impatiently waited for his treat. After just a few minutes, he heard someone call his name, and to his horror he saw one of his fellow members walking towards him. Just at that same moment, the waiter walked over, with a huge platter, holding a full roasted pig with an apple in its mouth. 'Isn't that something,' says the man after only a moment's pause, 'All I do is order an apple, and look what it comes with!'

"My wife went to a small village in mid Sussex"

"Newick?"

"No. Never heard of it before!"

Phil's nephew came to him with a problem. "I have my choice of two women," he said, "A beautiful, penniless young girl whom I love dearly, and a rich widow who I don't really love."

"Follow your heart; marry the girl you love," Phil counselled.

"Very well, Uncle Phil,' said the nephew, "That's sound advice."

"By the way," asked Phil "Where does the widow live?"

Chris and Colin were long-time neighbours in Nutley. Every time, Chris saw Colin coming round to his house, his heart sank. This was because he knew that, as always, Colin would be visiting him in order to borrow something and he was fed up with it.

"I'm not going to let Colin get away with it this time" he said quietly to his wife, "Watch what I'm about to do."

"Hi there, I wondered if you were thinking about using your hedge trimmer this afternoon?" asked Colin.

"Oh, I'm very sorry," said Chris, trying to look apologetic, 'but I'm actually going to be using it all this afternoon."

"In that case," responded Colin with a big grin, "You won't be using your golf clubs...mind if I borrow them?"

It was the day before the Battle of Hastings. King Harold asked his top man in the army, "Are my troops ready?"

"Yes, your Majesty", said the man, "Shall we give you a demonstration?"

"Yes, please", replied the King.

The man got all the archers lined up and instructed them to fire.

Thousand of arrows flew through the air and landed accurately.

However, one archer fired straight up into the air. The arrow flew up hundreds of feet, turned round and came back down again, landing just a few inches from where King Harold was standing.

"You want to watch him", said the King. "If he's not careful, he'll have somebody's eye out tomorrow!"

The Seven Dwarves were walking through the forest one day when they suddenly tumbled into a deep ravine. Snow White, who was following along behind her friends, stared over the edge of the ravine and called out to the dwarves. From the very depths of the dark hole, a voice came back, "Maidstone United will win the cup!"

Snow White heaved a sigh of relief, thinking "Well, at least Dopey's survived!"

How many Margate FC fans does it take to change a light bulb?

None, they're all happy living in the Bognor's shadow!

Supporters waiting to watch the latest Maidstone United vs Bognor Regis Town match heard that Maidstone were going to be delayed.

Apparently they saw a service station sign that said 'Clean Lavatories'...so they did.

What beverage do Margate Town players drink?

Penal-tea!

A man walked into a chip shop and said, "Hello. I'd like a steak and kiddely pie, please."

The woman behind the counter said, "What was that?"

"I'd like a steak and kiddely pie."

"I'm very sorry sir, what did you say?"

"I WANT A STEAK AND KIDDELY PIE!!"

"Do you mean 'steak and kidney' pie?"

"I said kiddely, diddle I?!"

(The steak and kidney pudding was first created in Sussex)

The nervous young batsman playing for Chiddingstone was having a very bad day. In a quieter moment in the game, he muttered to the one of his team mates, "Well, I suppose you've seen worse players." There was no response...so he said it again. "I said I guess you've seen worse players." His team mate looked at him and answered: "I heard you the first time. I was just trying to think..."

Two rival cricketers from Stonewell Park and Flimwell were having a chat. "The local team wants me to play for them very badly." said the man from Kent. "Well," said his friend, "You're just the man for the job."

A priest was walking along the Seven Sisters cliffs when he came upon two locals pulling a man from Kent ashore on the end of a rope.

"That's what I like to see," said the priest, "A man helping his fellow man."

As he was walking away, one local remarked to the other, "Well, he certainly doesn't know the first thing about shark fishing."

One day, a father and his son arrived at the ground to watch Dover RFC play Hove Rugby Club. But the man suddenly realised that he couldn't find their tickets for the game so he said to his son, "Nip home and see if I left the tickets there." His son replied "No probs, Dad." Half an hour later Bobby returned to his dad who was patiently waiting outside the ground and said, "Yep, they're on the kitchen table where you left them."

"Long, lazy Lewisham. little Lee,

Dirty Deptford, and Greenwich free."

"Starv'em, Rob'em, and Cheat'em

Stroud, Rochester and Chatham"

They say that a man from Kent laughs three times at a joke: the first time when everybody gets it, the second a week later when he thinks he gets it, the third time a month later when somebody explains it to him.

A man from Chichester went into a hardware store and asked to buy a sink.

"Would you like one with a plug?" asked the assistant.

"Don't tell me they've gone electric!" said the man.

A man from Maidstone bought two horses, but soon realised that he couldn't tell them apart. So he asked the farmer who lived next door what he should do. The farmer suggested he measure them.

The man came back triumphantly and said: "The white horse is two inches taller than the black horse!"

There are many good things to come out of Kent - most of them roads leading to Sussex.

Two blokes from Plaistow went into a pub.

The first man said "A pint o' bitter, and a half o' shandy for my mate 'Donkey', please!"

The publican replied "'What's with him calling you 'Donkey'?"

The second one said "Oh, 'e aw, 'e aw, 'e always calls me that!"

A couple from Kingston by Sea had been courting for nearly twenty years. One day as they sat on a seat in the park, the woman plucked up the courage to ask,

"Don't you think it's time we got married?"

Her sweetheart answered,

"Yes, but who'd have us?"

A rather cocky man working on a busy construction site in East Grinstead was bragging that he could outdo anyone in a feat of strength. He made a special case of making fun of Morris, one of the more senior workmen. After several minutes, Morris had had enough.

"Why don't you put your money where your mouth is?" he said. "I'll bet a week's wages that I can haul something in a wheelbarrow over to that outbuilding that you won't be able to wheel back."

"You're on, mate," the over confident young man replied. "It's a bet! Let's see what you got."

Morris reached out and grabbed the wheelbarrow by the handles. Then, nodding to the young man, he said, "All right. Get in."

Three friends, from Sussex University, the University of Kent and Oxford University respectively, were out having a good time together at a funfair. They were just about to go on the helter-skelter when a wise old woman stepped in front of them.

"This is a magic ride," she said. "You will land in whatever you shout out on the way down."

"I'm up for this," said the Sussex student and slid down the helter-skelter shouting "GOLD!" at the top of his voice. Sure enough, when he hit the bottom he found himself surrounded by thousands of pounds worth of gold coins.

The Oxford student went next and shouted "SILVER!" at the

top of his voice. At the bottom he landed in more silver coinage than he could even carry.

The Kent student went last and, launching himself from the top of the slide shouted "WEEEEEEE!"

A vicar from Sussex was travelling home one evening and was greatly annoyed when a man who was much the worse for drink, came and sat next to him on the bus.

"Young man," the vicar, declared in a rather pompous tone, "Do you not realise you are on the road to perdition?"

"Oh no!" replied the drunken man, "I could have sworn this bus went to Cuckfield."

At an antiques auction in Arundel, a wealthy American announced that he had lost his wallet containing £5,000, and he would give a reward of £50 to the person who found it. From the back of the hall a local man shouted, "I'll give £100!"

SUSSEX Wit & Humour

A man from Crawley was staggering home one evening, after a heavy night at the pub with his friends.

He suddenly noticed a man from the water board with a big 'T' handle, in the middle of the road opening a valve at the bottom of a manhole.

He walked up behind him and gave him a shove.

"What was that for?" asked the startled man.

The drunken man replied, "That's for turning all the streets round when I'm trying to find my way home!"

A farmer from Lewes once visited a farmer based in Ashford. The Lewes farmer asked "How big is your farm?" to which the other man replied "Can you see those trees over there? That's the boundary of my farmland'

The farmer responded, 'Wow. It takes me three days to drive to the boundary of my farm."

The man said "I had a car like that once."

Two men were waiting to be served in a butcher's shop in Bognor Regis. One of them said "I bet you £100 that you can't reach that piece of meat on the ceiling and the other man said "I'm not betting!". The first man asked "Why not?" and the other man replied "The steaks are too high!".

A farmer from Burnham Market was ploughing his field, he looked around and saw the vicar at the gate.

On next his circuit round he stopped to say hello.

"My, but you and God have built a beautiful place together" said the vicar.

"You're right, Vicar,' replied the Farmer, "But between you and me, you should have see it when he had it all to himself".

A life-long career man tired of his daily commute from Worthing to London decided he was going to give up his old life, move to the country, and become a chicken farmer. He bought on chicken farm in Bodiam and moved in. It turned out that his next door neighbour was also a chicken farmer. The neighbour came for a visit one day and said, "Chicken farming isn't easy you know. To help you get started, I'll give you 100 chickens."

The new chicken farmer was delighted. Two weeks later the neighbour dropped by to see how things were going. The new farmer said, "Not too well mate. All 100 chickens died." The neighbour said, "Oh, I can't believe that. I've never had any trouble with my chickens. I'll give you 100 more." Another two weeks went by and the neighbour dropped in again. The new farmer said, "You're not going to believe this, but the second 100 chickens died too." Astounded, the neighbour asked, "What went wrong?".

The new farmer said, "Well, I'm not sure whether I'm planting them too deep or too close together."

At a pub in Felpham, a newcomer asked a local man "Have you lived here all your life?"

After a long pause the man replied "Don't know yet!"

A tourist in a shop in Selsey asked the manager, "Have you got anything in the shape of motor car tyres?" The manager replied "Oh, yes. We've got lifebuoys, funeral wreaths and doughnuts."

A teacher at a school in Horsham was having a little trouble getting her year 11 pupils to understand grammar, 'These are what we call the pronouns', she said, 'And the way we use them with verbs; I am, you are, he/she is' she was saying, to glazed looks.

Trying a different tack she said, Lauren, give me a sentence with the pronoun, 'I' in it.'

Lauren began, 'I is...'

'No, no, no, no, no NO, NO!', shouted the teacher, 'Never, 'I is', always, 'I am'... now try again'.

Lauren looked puzzled and a little hurt, thought a while then began again more quietly,'I... am...the ninth letter of the alphabet'.

Have you heard about the latest machine at the arcades at Brighton?

You put ten pence in and ask it any question and it gives you a true answer.

One holiday maker from Dover tried it last week.

He asked the machine "Where is my father?" The machine replied:

"Your father is fishing in Herne Bay."

Well, he thought, that's daft for a start because my father is dead.

So he asked "Where is my mother's husband?"

The reply came back, "Your mother's husband is buried in Swale, but your father is still fishing in Herne Bay."

A man and his wife walked past a fancy new restaurant in Horsham.

... "Did you smell that food?" the woman asked... "Wonderful!"

Being the kind hearted, generous man that he was, her husband thought,

"What the hell, I'll treat her!"

So they walked past it a second time.

Many years ago there was a dispute between two villages, one in Sussex and the other in Kent; one day the villagers heard the cry "One Sussex man is stronger than one hundred Kent men."

The villagers in Kent were furious and immediately sent their 100 strongest men to engage with the enemy; they were horrified by the screams and shouts. After hours of fighting all was quiet and no-one returned.

Later the same voice shouted out, "Is that the best you can do?"

This fired up the people from Kent and they rallied round and got together 1000 men to do battle; after days of the most frightful blood curling sounds one man emerged from the battlefield, barely able to speak, but with his last breath managed to murmur "It's a trap, there's two of them!".

Did you hear about the last wish of the henpecked husband of a house-proud wife?

He asked to have his ashes scattered on the carpet.

Did you hear about the truck driver from Ardingly who was seen desperately chiselling away at the brickwork after his lorry got stuck at the entrance of a tunnel?

"Why don't you let some air out of your tyres?" asked a helpful passer-by.

"No, mate," replied the driver "It's the roof that won't go under, not the wheels."

It was a quiet night in Copthorne and a man and his wife were fast asleep when there was an unexpected knock on the door. The man looked at his alarm clock. It was half past three in the morning. "I'm not getting out of bed at this time," he thought and rolled over.

A louder knock followed. "Aren't you going to answer that?" asked his wife.

So the man dragged himself out of bed and went downstairs. He opened the door to find a strange man standing at the door. It didn't take the homeowner long to realise the man was drunk.

"Hi there," slurred the stranger. "Can you give me a push?"

"No, I'm sorry. It's half past three. I was in bed," said the man and slammed the door. He went back up to bed and told his wife what happened.

"That wasn't very nice of you," she said.

"Remember that night we broke down in the pouring rain on the way to pick the kids up from the babysitter, and you had to knock on that man's door to get us started again? What would have happened if he'd told us to get lost?"

"But the man who just knocked on our door was drunk," replied her husband.

"Well, we can at least help move his car somewhere safe and sort him out a taxi," said his wife. "He needs our help." So the husband got out of bed again, got dressed, and went downstairs. He opened the door, but couldn't to see the stranger anywhere so he shouted, "Hey, do you still want a push?". In answer, he heard a voice call out, "Yes please!" So, still being unable to see the stranger, he shouted,

"Where are you?"

"I'm over here," the stranger replied, "on your swing."

A school pupil from Uckfield asked his teacher, "Are 'trousers' singular or plural?"

The teacher replied, "They're singular on top and plural on the bottom."

A man from Hailsham said to his wife, "Get your coat on love. I'm off to the club".

His wife said, "That's nice. You haven't taken me out for years".

He said, "You're not coming with me...I'm turning the heating off when I go out".

A farmer was driving along a country road in the South Downs with a large load of fertiliser. A little boy, playing on front of his house, saw him and called, "What do you have in your truck?"

"Fertiliser," the farmer replied.

"What are you going to do with it?" asked the little boy.

"Put it on strawberries," answered the farmer.

"You ought to live here," the little boy advised him. 'We put sugar and cream on ours."

Pete and Larry hadn't seen each other in many years. They were having a long chat, telling each other all about their lives. Finally Pete invited Larry to visit him in his new apartment in Eastbourne. "I have a wife and three kids and I'd love to have you visit us."

"Great. Where do you live?"

"Here's the address. There's plenty of parking behind the flat. Park and come around to the front door, kick it open with your foot, go to the elevator and press the button with your left elbow, then enter! When you reach the sixth floor, go down the hall until you see my name on the door. Then press the doorbell with your right elbow and I'll let you in."

"Great. But tell me...what is all this business of kicking the front door open, then pressing elevator buttons with my right, then my left elbow?"

Pete answered, "Surely you're not coming empty-handed?"

Sam worked in an office in Crawley. One day he walked into his boss's office and said, "I'll be honest with you, I know the economy isn't great, but I have three companies after me, and I would like to respectfully ask for a pay rise."

After a few minutes of haggling, his manager finally agreed to a 5% pay rise, and Sam happily got up to leave.

"By the way", asked the boss as Sam got up, "Which three companies are after you?"

"The electric company, the water company, and the phone company", Sam replied.

A man from East Wittering wanted to become a monk so he went to the monastery and talked to the head monk.

The head monk said, "You must take a vow of silence and can only say two words every three years."

The man agreed and after the first three years, the head monk came to him and said, "What are your two words?"

"Food cold!" the man replied.

Three more years went by and the head monk came to him and said "What are your two words?"

"Robe dirty!" the man exclaimed.

Three more years went by and the head monk came to him and said, "What are your two words?"

"I quit!" said the man.

"Well", the head monk replied, "I'm not surprised. You've done nothing but complain ever since you got here!"

A lawyer from Kent and a businessman from Sussex ended up sitting next to each other on a flight to the airport.

The lawyer started thinking that he could have some fun at the businessman's expense and asked him if he'd like to play a game. The businessman was tired and just wanted to relax. He politely declined the offer and tried to sleep. The lawyer persisted, explaining:

"I ask you a question, and if you don't know the answer, you pay me only £5; you ask me one, and if I don't know the answer, I will pay you £500."

This got the businessman a little more interested and he finally agreed to play the game.

The lawyer asked the first question, "What's the distance from the Earth to the moon?"

The Sussex man said nothing, but reached into his pocket, pulled out a five-pound note and handed it to the lawyer.

Now, it was his turn. He asked the lawyer, "What goes up a hill with three legs, and comes down with four?"

The lawyer used his laptop. He used the air-phone; he searched the web, he sent emails to his most well read friends, but still came up with nothing. After over an hour of searching, he finally gave up.

He woke up the businessman and handed him £500. The man smugly pocketed the cash and went straight back to sleep.

The lawyer went wild with curiosity and wanted to know the answer. He woke the businessman up and asked, "Well? What goes up a hill with three legs and comes down with four?"

The businessman reached into his pocket, handed the lawyer £5 and went back to sleep.

Two elderly ladies were enjoying a half pint of shandy in the Black Rabbit pub in Arundel. One said to the other, "Was it love at first sight when you met your old man?"" No I don't think so," came the reply,

"I didn't know how much money he had when I first met him!"

Jim, a man from Crowborough, got onto the bus with his hands held out in front of him about a foot apart. The conductor came up to him and said, "Give us your fare, Jim!" "I can't" replied Jim. "I'll pay you on the way back." The conductor looked puzzled and said, "I'll get the sack if the inspector gets on. I've got to have your fare now!". "That's nothing to what I'll get when I go home" answered Jim "And I have to tell the missus to re measure the window I bust this morning!"

A bloke walked up to the foreman of a road laying gang in Hailsham and asked for a job. "I haven't got one for you today." said the foreman looking up from his newspaper. "But if you walk half a mile down here, you can see if you like the work and I can put you on the list for tomorrow."That's great mate," said the bloke as he wandered off down the road to find the gang. At the end of the shift, the man walked past the foreman and shouted, "Thanks mate. See you tomorrow." The foreman looked up from his paper and shouted back, "You've enjoyed yourself then?". "Yes I have!" shouted back the bloke, " But can I have a shovel or a pick to lean on like the rest of the gang?".

A labourer shouted up to his roofer mate on top of an old terraced house in Steyning, saying, "Don't start climbing down this ladder, Burt." "Why not?" Burt called back. "Cos I moved it five minutes ago!" replied his mate.

A visitor from Kent was driving his fancy new car around Bexhill and found that he was lost. The driver stopped old Tom and said, "You there! Old man, what happens if I turn left here?" "Don't know sir," replied old Tom.

"Well what if I turn right here, where will that take me?" continued the visitor. "Don't know sir." replied old Tom.

Becoming fed up, the driver continued, "Well, what if I go straight on?" A flicker of knowledge moved over old Tom's face until he replied, "Don't know sir." "I say old man you don't know a lot do you?" retorted the posh bloke.

Old Tom looked at him and said, "I may not know a lot but I ain't lost like you are!" With that, old Tom walked off leaving the motorist stranded.

Harry proudly drove his new convertible into town and parked it on the main street he was on his way to the recycling centre to get rid of an unwanted gift, a foot spa, which he left on the back seat.

He had walked half way down the street when he realised that he had left the top down... with the foot spa in the back.

He ran all the way back to his car, but it was too late...

Another five foot spas had been dumped in the car.

What gear were you in at the moment of the impact?

Gucci sweats and Reeboks.

Two aerials meet on a roof - fall in love - get married. The ceremony was rubbish - but the reception was brilliant.

A duck walks into a pub and goes up to the barman.

The barman says 'What can I get you?'

Duck: 'Umm. Do you have any grapes?'

Barman (Looking surprised):

'No, I'm afraid we don't.'

The duck waddles slowly out of the pub.

The next day at the same time, the duck waddles into the pub, hops up on a bar stool.

Barman: 'Hi. What can I get for you?'

Duck: 'Um. Do you have any grapes?'

Barman (a little annoyed): 'Hey! Weren't you in here yesterday. Look mate, we don't have any grapes. OK?'

The duck hops off the stool and waddles out of the door.

The next day, at the same time, the barman is cleaning some glasses when he hears a familiar voice

Duck: 'Umm.. Do you have any grapes?'

The barman is really annoyed

Barman: 'Look. What's your problem? You came in here yesterday asking for grapes, I told you, we don't have any grapes! Next time I see your little ducktail waddle in here I'm going to nail those little webbed feet of yours to the floor. GOT me pal?'

So the duck hops off the bar stool and waddles out.

The next day at the same time, the duck waddles into the pub, walks up to the barman and the barman says,

'What on earth do YOU want?'

'Errrr. do you have any nails?'

'What!? Of course not.'

'Oh. Well, do you have any grapes?'

A new client had just come in to see a famous lawyer.

'Can you tell me how much you charge?', said the client.

'Of course', the lawyer replied, 'I charge £200 to answer three questions!'

'Well that's a bit steep, isn't it?'

'Yes it is,' said the lawyer, 'And what's your third question?'

A passenger in a taxi tapped the driver on the shoulder to ask him something.

The driver screamed, lost control of the cab, nearly hit a bus, drove up

over the curb and stopped just inches from a large plate glass window.

For a few moments everything was silent in the cab, then the driver said, 'Please, don't ever do that again. You scared the daylights out of me.'

The passenger, who was also frightened, apologised and said he didn't realize that a tap on the shoulder could frighten him so much, to which the driver replied, 'I'm sorry, it's really not your fault at all. Today is my first day driving a cab. I've been driving a hearse for the last 25 years.'

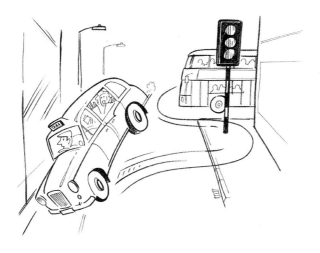

Unusual Sussex place names

Balls Cross

Batchelor's Bump

Beggars Bush

Cackle Street

Cocking

Crapham Down

Crazy Lane

Lickfold

Lower Dicker